Succe

A Biblical Exploration

Simon Coupland

Team Vicar in Broadwater Parish, Worthing

GROVE BOOKS LIMITED
RIDLEY HALL RD CAMBRIDGE CB3 9HU

Contents

Acknowledgements

My thanks to Chichester diocese for a sabbatical month in which to undertake the research behind this booklet, to my colleagues at Broadwater and especially Queen Street Fellowship for covering for me during my absence, and to the Ridley Hall staff and Grove Spirituality group for our fruitful discussions.

The Cover Illustration is by Peter Ashton

First Impression May 2002
ISSN 0262-799X
ISBN 1 85174 497 5

Introduction

1

As a Christian, and especially as a Christian minister, I am conscious of treading a fine line between the acceptance of failure and the desire for success.

Take the parable of the sower (Mark 4), for instance. Some read it and emphasize the costly reality of discipleship—Jesus warns that we will face three failures for every success. Others read it and point to the amazing fruitfulness that Jesus predicted—thirty, sixty, even a hundred fold! Where does the right balance lie?

The same tension is apparent when it comes to the church. It is easy to be conscious of failure when we read the almost gleeful reports in the secular press of attendance declining and churches closing, and when we see the progressive loss of influence of the Christian faith in our society. When I get together with other clergy (and I suspect the laity are not that different) I can quickly become disheartened when everyone else's church seems to be bigger than mine or growing faster than mine, and I can easily fall into the trap of trying to find something to boast about in return.

We follow one whose ministry ended not in popularity and triumph, but on a cross

In our feelings of frustration and failure, we may remind ourselves that we follow one whose ministry ended not in popularity and triumph, but on a cross. As Bonhoeffer wrote, 'the figure of the Crucified invalidates all thought which takes success for its standard.'[1] And so when we look at falling church attendance or our precarious bank balance we may comfort ourselves with the thought that we are not called to success, only to faithfulness.[2] I well remember being told at the start of a university mission that the important thing was not how many were converted, but that the gospel was preached—we should not play the numbers game.

Yet does this attitude show too great a willingness to embrace failure, emphasizing the barren soil, the shallow roots and the choking weeds at the expense of the crop which we should also be looking to harvest? Tom Wright has argued that 'it is impossible to justify churches that really are failing, failing in their witness to a pagan society, on the grounds that failure is what

Christianity is all about.'[3] The cross was, after all, not the last word in Jesus' life—it was followed by resurrection, ascension and glorious reign at the Father's right hand. So perhaps there is a need to redress the balance, particularly if, as Richard Higginson suspects, 'the British tend to be suspicious of successful people—and so do many Christians.'[4]

We can detect a desire to reverse this negative trend, to celebrate success, to raise the church's profile and to reach the nation for Christ behind several strategies which have made a significant impact in recent years. *March for Jesus* is one example, *Alpha* another. Both seek to bring Christians together in a positive way to proclaim the gospel, and both have grown from small beginnings to enjoy huge success around the globe. Neither is embarrassed by its success; on the contrary, in their publicity material both have emphasized their remarkable growth and the hope of growing still further.

Sanctified Success?

Not everyone is happy about this positive approach. According to one critic, there is among charismatic Christians an unhealthy emphasis on success, albeit with 'a sanctifying Christian tag to it.'[5] Roland Howard claims that

> 'Holy success is seen in the accomplishment of psychological integration, health, beauty, good relationships and, sometimes, wealth …The idea is that with God and the correct instructions, Christians can find fulfilment and success.'

He sees the evidence for this in Christian magazines, with their 'aspirational success-orientated values,' in the 'scores of Christian "How-to" books' and in the promotion of Christian celebrities such as Cliff Richard, Delia Smith or Jonathan Edwards. If this represents one person's controversial opinion, it is clear that one branch of the evangelical church has overtly and unapologetically embraced success-oriented teaching, namely the Faith Movement with its so-called 'health and wealth gospel.' For example, one of its proponents, Kenneth Hagin, has written,

> '[God] wants his children to eat the best, he wants them to wear the best clothing, he wants them to drive the best cars, and he wants them to have the best of everything.'[6]

But is this a success too far? Where does the right balance lie? All of which prompts the question, what *is* success? What do we mean by the term? A moment's reflection shows that it means different things in different areas of life. In financial terms, success is prosperity. In military terms, it is victory. In developmental terms, maturity. In popular terms, celebrity. And in Christian terms? That is the question which this booklet will address. As a Christian, and more particularly a Christian whose faith is moulded by and based upon the Bible, what does it mean to be successful? Is it even an appropriate goal when we follow a crucified Saviour? For those who are called to take up their cross daily, is it right to look for success, and if so, what kind of success?

Is success an appropriate goal when we follow a crucified Saviour?

To answer these questions, we will turn first and foremost to Scripture. We will not find the word 'success' very often in Old or New Testament (in any Bible translations), so we need to look for a range of goals or outcomes which are presented as successes—accomplishments, achievements or behaviour held up as praiseworthy in the eyes of the writers or, more especially, God. First we will look briefly at Old Testament models of success and failure, where we will discover a certain degree of ambiguity. We will go on to consider Jesus' ministry, asking the question, 'was it a failure or a success?' and pose the same question in relation to Paul's ministry. We will then turn to the teaching of Jesus, seeking to discern what Jesus had to say about success and failure. In particular, we will consider four main strands in his teaching which relate to success in this life or the next: heavenly reward; greatness; fruitfulness; and victory. Finally, we will attempt to relate all this to everyday life for the twenty-first-century Christian—what does it mean for us to be successful, if indeed that is an appropriate aim?

2

Success in the Old Testament

We do not have space here to consider the whole of the Old Testament, but it is nonetheless helpful to look briefly at some of the currents which are found there, especially as these do not all flow in the same direction.

For example, the book of Deuteronomy seems to offer support to a prosperity gospel. Look at chapter 28: 'All these blessings will come upon you and accompany you if you obey the LORD your God…The LORD will grant you abundant prosperity—in the fruit of your womb, the young of your livestock and the crops of your ground' (28.2, 11). Or again, in chapter 30, we find the promise that even when the people of Israel turn away from the Lord, if they return to him, 'He will make you more prosperous and numerous than your fathers' (30.5). So we find in Deuteronomy the promise of success, not only in the shape of prosperity and fertility, as here, but also victory in battle (6.18–19; 20.1–4) and fame among the nations (4.5–8).

By contrast, Maria Boulding has highlighted the way in which some of the great prophets of the Old Testament were called to rejection and failure, including Hosea, Isaiah and Jeremiah: 'Failure was explicitly built into their mission.'[7] Thus Isaiah was told, 'Make the heart of this people calloused; make their ears dull and close their eyes. Otherwise they might see with their eyes, hear with their ears, understand with their hearts, and turn and be healed' (Is. 6.9–10). Right at the outset of his ministry Isaiah is thus warned that his mission is doomed to fail, however obedient he is to the Law or to his calling. Similarly, Jeremiah is given the message to proclaim: '"From the time your forefathers left Egypt until now, day after day, again and again I sent you my servants the prophets. But they did not listen to me or pay attention."…When you tell them all this, they will not listen to you' (Jer. 7.25–27). True, in one sense Jeremiah is upholding the Deuteronomic perspective, in that he is telling the people that they are paying the penalty for turning their backs on God. But in personal terms he is explicitly forewarned that he can never be successful, because the people will never listen. This is a truly unenviable ministry!

> *Some of the great Old Testament prophets were called to rejection and failure*

Another relevant Old Testament book is Job, whose main purpose seems to be to undermine the theology of obedience and reward. Again and again Job insists, against the relentless pressure of his counsellors, that he is suffering without cause, a stance which is upheld by the narrator. Although this might appear to be subverted by the end of the book, where Job receives back twice as much as he had enjoyed before (42.10–17), commentators underline that this is not a simple return to a theology of retribution. Rather, 'this act of restoration is an act of grace, not a reward for Job's goodness or honesty with God.'[8] Not surprisingly, teachers from the Faith Movement see the book in a different light. They argue that Job brought his troubles upon himself by his fear (3.25), a 'negative confession' which removed God's hedge of protection (1.10) around him. When Job repented of his fear and prayed for his friends, God restored his prosperity.[9] Where the book goes against this interpretation, as for example when Job says, 'The LORD gave and the LORD has taken away' (1.21), the words are said to be neither true nor inspired.[10] In this way those who proclaim the gospel of health and wealth align themselves with Job's comforters rather than with Job himself.

Those who proclaim the gospel of health and wealth align themselves with Job's comforters

The Challenge of Meaninglessness

Even more challenging to the doctrine of retribution is Ecclesiastes. The author, named in Hebrew *Qoheleth*, 'the Teacher,' is a success story, someone who could say, with Byron, 'Drank every cup of joy, heard every trump of fame; drank early; deeply drank; drank draughts which common millions might have drunk.' As one commentator remarks, 'He built for himself his own secure world, with all the marks of what we normally consider worldly success.'[11] And yet *Qoheleth* would also echo Byron's conclusion: 'Then died of thirst, because there was no more to drink.' In the end, he says, all is empty and meaningless, *hebel*. This is set out as a rule of life in 9.11: 'The race is not to the swift or the battle to the strong, nor does food come to the wise or wealth to the brilliant or favour to the learned; but time and chance happen to them all.' And yet alongside this negativity, a positive thread runs throughout the book: 'A man can do nothing better than to eat and drink and find satisfaction in his work. This too, I see, is from the hand of God' (2.24; see also 3.12–13; 5.18; 8.15; 9.7–9). Success can thus be a good thing, but only in the right perspective. By itself it is meaningless, but success enjoyed is the best we can find in this life.

...ccess can be a good ...ing, but only in the right perspective

It is fascinating to note that a contemporary book for managers, *The Paradox of Success*, contains a very similar message from a purely secular perspective.[12] The author urges business leaders to recognize that success has a dark and self-destructive side, and that those who are going to enjoy success in the long term need to adopt a balanced lifestyle and, interestingly, an ethical framework.

In sum, there is no single attitude to success in the Old Testament, but a range of views, some of them apparently formulated as a conscious moderation or modification of others. This should warn us against quoting verses or passages out of context to support an argument without acknowledging that other parts of Scripture represent a very different viewpoint. Moreover, as Christians we are also obliged to balance the teaching of the Old Testament with that of the New.[13] This is of particular importance when it comes to God's promise of material blessing. Jacques Ellul has argued that under the old covenant, wealth was a type of 'sacrament,' only to be stripped of that sacramental character by Jesus, who became in himself the believer's true and only wealth. 'Wealth, then, is reduced to money. And money has no place in the work of redemption.'[14] This is a theme to which we shall return.

3

Jesus: Success or Failure?

Several of those who have written about success and failure have pointed to the cross as a supreme example of the latter.

I have already quoted Bonhoeffer; in a similar vein, Maria Boulding calls her chapter on Jesus, 'The Failed Messiah,' and says memorably: 'The Word was made failure and died among us.'[15] Or here is Paul Tournier: 'After the proof of God by success, there comes the proof of God in failure.'[16] Yet is this an accurate reflection of the gospels' perspective? In this section we will examine the evidence, and suggest that the New Testament portrays the whole of Jesus' ministry, including his death on the cross, as a success, even though this necessarily entails revising our criteria of success and failure.

Clearly the first part of Jesus' ministry is portrayed by all the gospel writers as a success story, as Tournier emphasizes in the quotation above. In his healings, his casting out of demons, his pronouncements of forgiveness, his authority over nature, and in the preaching of good news to the poor we see a man of authority, power and success. The measure of this success is highlighted by the rare failure at Nazareth, where 'he could not do any miracles, except lay his hands on a few sick people and heal them' (Mark 6.5; Matthew 13.54–8). Significantly, Mark immediately follows this episode with the sending out of the Twelve, who meet with great success as they travel through the rest of Galilee: 'They drove out many demons and

The measure of his success is highlighted by the failure at Nazareth

anointed many sick people with oil and healed them' (6.12–13). Another reflection of the success of Jesus' ministry is the way in which the evangelists present him as a new Moses and a new Elijah.[17] These two larger-than-life Old Testament characters had their fair share of flaws and failures, but exercised ministries of great power and remarkable success.[18] Their appearance with Jesus at the Transfiguration sealed the bond between them.

The Shock of Failure

If Jesus' prowess as healer and miracle-worker led his followers to expect even greater successes when they reached Jerusalem, his arrest, trial and crucifixion came as a shock and a failure. They had failed to understand Jesus' predictions of rejection and suffering, they failed to see any fulfilment of Scripture in the events of Good Friday, and even on the third day after the event they were still deep in confusion and despair (Luke 24.19–21). From their perspective at the time, the cross was unquestionably a failure, which is why Boulding, like Tournier above, writes of 'a contrast…between the two phases of Jesus' ministry: the earlier one in Galilee, when he was on the whole successful, and the later one in Jerusalem which was consummated by failure.'[19] For pagan and Jewish authors outside the early Christian movement, Jesus was consequently nothing more than another failed Messiah 'whose botched career ended in tragedy.'[20] Yet a closer look reveals that the gospel writers (and indeed the other New Testament writers) do not portray the crucifixion as a failure.

Mark offers the bleakest picture of the crucifixion. The scene is one of darkness and dereliction (15.33–4), so that Walter Moberly has likened it to Grünewald's Isenheim altarpiece, on which the twisted, scarred body of Jesus hangs in agony.[21] Here indeed appears to be a portrayal of failure. Matthew largely follows Mark, but the picture in Luke is very different. Here Jesus speaks words of forgiveness and salvation (23.34, 43), and whereas in

Mark his last utterance is simply described as a loud cry (15.37), Luke records words of faith and assurance: 'Father, into your hands I commit my spirit' (23.46). Luke thus depicts Jesus as a man who even *in extremis* is in control, who speaks in death, as in life, with confident authority. Moberly compares the scene to the peaceful and dignified portrayals of the crucifixion by Fra Angelico.

John likewise offers a positive picture of the cross. This is where Jesus is glorified (12.23, 28; 13.31–2), where he bears much fruit (12.24) and where he is lifted up to draw all people to himself (12.32–3; see also 3.14–15; 8.28). Whereas in the synoptic gospels Jesus appears to be abandoned and alone, with some women 'watching from a distance' (Mark 15.40), in John they are 'near the cross' (19.25), near enough for Jesus to be able to speak to them, and accompanied by 'the disciple whom Jesus loved.' The soldiers dice for his robe and Jesus is thirsty, 'so that the Scripture would be fulfilled' (19.24, 28).

The cross in John is not the place of failure, but the place of triumph

All that happens has to happen, as has been prophesied long before. And as many a preacher has commented, Jesus' last word is one of fulfilment, of completion: 'Tetelestai'—'It is finished' (19.28). The cross in John is thus not the place of failure, but the place of triumph, exaltation and glory.[22]

The Greatest Triumph

Yet further reflection shows that the same is true of all the synoptic Gospels, not just Luke. Thus in Mark (echoed in Matthew) Jesus three times predicts that the Son of Man must die, but will be raised (Mark 8.31; 9.31; 10.33–4) and tells the disciples precisely why he has come: 'to give his life as a ransom for many' (10.45). In the parable of the vineyard he predicts the death of the owner's son as a necessary preliminary to his subsequent vindication (12.1–12). At the last supper he speaks of his broken body and 'blood of the covenant, which is poured out for many' (14.22–5). And to the high priest he declares confidently, in an allusion to the vindication scene of Daniel 7: 'You will see the Son of Man sitting at the right hand of the Mighty One and coming on the clouds of heaven' (14.62). All this makes plain that even if the disciples did not understand what was going on, Jesus did, and more significantly, that Mark wants his readers to understand, too. Just as the prologue to each gospel gives the reader the narrative keys with which to interpret what follows,[23] so all these hints and clues are intended to prepare us for the cross and, to some extent, explain its significance. All this is underlined when Jesus dies. The curtain of the temple is 'torn in two from top to bottom' and the watching centurion declares, 'Surely this man was the Son of God!' (15.38–9). In Matthew the point is made even more forcefully, as 'the tombs broke open and the bodies of many holy people who had died were raised to life' (27.52). This is clearly no failure! Even if Jesus' followers could not yet perceive it, Matthew and Mark, like Luke and John, want their readers to recognize that this is the greatest triumph the world has ever seen.

This is of course also the perspective of the rest of the New Testament. Through the cross 'we have redemption, the forgiveness of sins' (Ephesians 1.7); through the cross 'we have confidence to enter the Most Holy Place' (Hebrews 10.19); on the cross Jesus 'reconciled both [Jew and Gentile] to God, putting to death their hostility' (Ephesians 2.14–16); on the cross he 'cancelled the written code, with its regulations…and made a public spectacle of the powers and authorities' (Colossians 3.14–15); on the cross he 'purchased men for God from every tribe and language and people and nation' (Revelation 5.9). These references—and I could quote many more—demonstrate that the notion that the first half of Jesus' ministry was a success, followed by the failure of the cross, or indeed that the cross was a failure, redeemed by the resurrection, is quite alien to the New Testament writers.[24]

Having said that, the cross clearly redefines the whole concept of success. This is a theme to which we shall return, but it is important to emphasize that the perspective of the gospel writers, and of course of Jesus himself, is not necessarily the same as that of the secular world. As Paul said, 'We preach Christ crucified: a stumbling-block to Jews and foolishness to Gentiles, but to those whom God has called, both Jews and Greeks, Christ the power of God and the wisdom of God' (1 Corinthians 1.23–4). Yet some prosperity teaching wants to rob the cross of its

The cross clearly redefines the whole concept of success

offence. For example, Robert Schuller says, '[Jesus] bore the cross to sanctify your self-esteem. The cross will sanctify the ego trip.'[25] Others argue that because Jesus suffered, we no longer have to.[26] This is a travesty of the New Testament, which teaches that as we take up our cross daily (Luke 9.23), 'the sufferings of Christ flow over into our lives' (2 Corinthians 1.5).

Paul: Success or Failure?

It might be thought that, by any standards, Paul's ministry was an outstanding success. Yet in 2 Corinthians, Paul himself apparently speaks of weakness and suffering as the defining characteristics of his apostleship. Maria Boulding sees this as central to his self-understanding: 'Paul's weakness and failures are the place where the power of the risen Christ can shine unhindered; they are therefore necessary to his ministry.'[27] In chapters 11 and 12 of the letter Paul certainly seems to say that the true greatness of an apostle is measured by suffering: 'Are they servants of Christ? (I am out of my mind to talk like this.) I am more.' Then, when we might expect him to list the number of people he has brought to Christ, the number of churches he has planted, the number of leaders he has nurtured, he goes on: 'I have worked much harder, been in prison more frequently, been flogged more severely, and been exposed to death again and again' (2 Corinthians 11.23). This is a harsh yardstick for ministerial 'success'—and one which very few church leaders in the West today would match up to!

Yet we must recognize that Paul's arguments in 2 Corinthians are rhetorical, even if there is truth behind them. We can be sure of this because in the very same passage he describes other 'things that mark an apostle,' namely 'signs, wonders and miracles' (12.12). And elsewhere in the letter he describes the members of the church themselves as 'our letter, written on our hearts, known and read by everybody…the result of our ministry' (2 Corinthians 3.2–3). In other words, Paul regards the true measure of his success as the success of the gospel, souls won for Christ. Thus the believers at Philippi are his 'joy and crown' (Philippians 4.1), and to the Christians in Rome he writes, 'I will not venture to speak of anything except what Christ has accomplished through me in leading the Gentiles to obey God by what I have said and done—by the power of signs and miracles, through the power of the Spirit. So from Jerusalem all the way round to Illyricum, I have fully proclaimed the gospel of Christ. It has always been my ambition to preach the gospel where Christ was not known, so that I would not be building on someone else's foundation' (Romans 15.18–20). Here we see Paul reflecting on his apostolic ministry without rhetoric or irony. His accomplishment, his achievement,[28] is what Christ has accomplished through him—men and women coming to faith. His ambition (another indication of what he views as success) is to take the gospel to new places.

Paul's accomplishment is what Christ has accomplished through him

A quite different, more personal definition of success is found in 2 Timothy—fighting the good fight, finishing the race, keeping the faith. And the reward for success will be 'the crown of righteousness, which the Lord, the righteous Judge, will award to me on that day' (2 Timothy 4.7–8). In short, we must read Paul's words in 2 Corinthians in the context of the rest of his writings. The measure of his success was not his sufferings in themselves, but his proclamation of the gospel, which caused those sufferings, and his faithful perseverance, which meant sharing Christ's sufferings. Yet those sufferings were not in any sense 'failure'; that is not how he ever described them. 'Weaknesses,' yes, with 'insults, hardships, persecutions and difficulties' (2 Corinthians 12.10), but not failures, merely part of what it means as a Christian to 'fill up in [one's] flesh what is still lacking in regard to Christ's afflictions, for the sake of his body, which is the church' (Colossians 1.24).

Jesus Redefines Success (1): Wealth and Greatness

4

As a look at any Bible concordance will show, Jesus did not explicitly talk about 'success.'

But as was said earlier, in his teaching Jesus spoke in various ways about accomplishment or fulfilment, and a study of the gospels reveals four main strands to this teaching, which we shall look at in turn.

Worldly Wealth and Treasure in Heaven

The first strand relates to prosperity. If one obvious criterion for success in life is wealth, Jesus turns that on its head by telling his disciples, 'Do not store up for yourselves treasures on earth…But store up for yourselves treasures in heaven' (Matt. 6.19–20; also Matt. 19.21; Mark 10.21; Luke 12.33; 18.22). This notion of reward, often but not always specified as a heavenly one, is a prominent theme in his teaching, particularly in the synoptic Gospels. There are direct references, such as in the Sermon on the Mount, where Jesus promises 'great reward in heaven' to various groups of people. These include those who are persecuted for his sake (Matt. 5.12; Luke 6.23), those who fast, pray or give alms in secret (Matt. 6.4, 6, 18), and those who receive a prophet or a righteous man, or even give a cup of cold water to 'one of these little ones' (Matthew 10.41–2). There are several parables which promise reward for faithful service, including the talents and pounds (Matt. 25.14–30; Luke 19.11–27), the master and servants (Matt. 24.45–7; Luke 12.35–8, 42–4) or the rich man and Lazarus (Luke 16.19–31, especially v 25). Jesus' own role in apportioning these rewards comes across not only in the parable of the sheep and goats (Matthew 25.31–46) but also in Matthew 16.27: 'The Son of Man is going to come in his Father's glory with his angels, and will then reward each person according to what he has done.'

The parable of the talents (Matt. 25.14–30) is of particular interest. First, it underlines the fact that the Christian life, like life in general, is not a level playing field. Some have ten talents, some five, and some just one. This does not provide grounds for complaint or cause for sympathy, it is simply a fact. As a result it is pointless, if not downright unhelpful, to compare ourselves with

The master wants to know how well we have done with what we have been given

others, because what the master wants to know is how well we have done with what we have been given. Fred Smith, a Christian businessman, comments: 'The person doing the most with what he's got is truly successful. Not the one who becomes the richest or most famous, but the one who has the closest ratio of talents received to talents used.'[29] Second, Jesus implies that there are degrees of heavenly reward. This might seem to run counter to the parable of the workers in the vineyard, who all get the same pay no matter how long they work (Matt. 20.1–16), but Paul's housebuilding metaphor in 1 Corinthians 3.10–15 provides a useful analogy. Paul says that anyone who builds on the foundation of Jesus will be saved, but some will receive additional reward on the basis of the way in which they have lived. Salvation for all the workers in the vineyard; additional reward for those to whom the master can say: 'Well done, good and faithful servant!'[30]

Prosperity

Another noteworthy passage is Jesus' response to Peter's typically brash outburst, 'We have left everything to follow you! What then will there be for us?' All three synoptic gospels agree that Jesus promised 'many times as much in this age and, in the age to come, eternal life' (Luke 18.28–30; Mark 10.28–30), but Matthew adds an additional reward: 'At the renewal of all things, when the Son of Man sits on his glorious throne, you who have followed me will also sit on twelve thrones, judging the twelve tribes of Israel' (Matt. 19.27–9; also Luke 22.29–30). This is unusual in being the only passage, apart from the story of the rich man and Lazarus,[31] to specify what a heavenly reward, or treasure in heaven, might consist of. But this reward is evidently specific to the apostles so it leaves us little wiser as to what Jesus' followers would have understood by 'treasure in heaven.'[32] John Stott comments, 'What is this? Jesus does not explain.'[33] Equally remarkable is the fact that it is the only passage which promises reward in this life as well as in the age to come. So teachers in the prosperity movement have seized upon it, dubbing it the 'hundredfold return' after Jesus' pledge that 'no-one...will fail to receive a hundred times as much' (Mark 10.30; also Matt. 19.29). Gloria Copeland explains,

What is this 'treasure in heaven'? Jesus does not explain

> 'You give $1 for the gospel's sake and $100 belongs to you; give $10 and receive $1000; give $1000 and receive $100,000...Give one house and receive one hundred houses or one house worth one hundred times as much...Give one car and the return would furnish you a lifetime of cars. In short, Mark 10.30 is a very good deal.'[34]

It is easy to see why Copeland quotes Mark rather than Luke; Luke makes no reference to houses and fields and clearly understood Jesus' promise to refer to a spiritual rather than physical return, since it is unlikely that the disciples were promised additional wives and parents! Yet Luke was merely bringing out what was implicit in Matthew and Mark, since the same reference to 'brothers, sisters, mothers and children' is found there, too. More significant is what Copeland has omitted to quote from Mark 10.30: 'and with them, persecutions.' This is part of the 'good deal' which she fails to mention! Here, then, as in the rest of the gospels, Jesus' teaching represents a marked contrast to Deuteronomy. He guarantees blessing not 'in the fruit of your womb, the young of your livestock and the crops of your ground' (Deuteronomy 28.11), but with the Father in the heavenly kingdom. Success for the Christian cannot therefore be measured in terms of worldly prosperity; indeed, Jesus calls the poor 'blessed' (Luke 6.20).

This sets Jesus' teaching in sharp contrast to the prosperity gospel of the Faith Movement, which promises God's people success not only in terms of heavenly riches, but also the best here on earth. The title of Gloria Copeland's book says it all: *God's Will is Prosperity*. To show how she applies her teaching in her own life, she relates what she did when she wanted a new house: 'I began to see that I already had authority over that house and authority over the money I needed to purchase it. I said, "In the Name of Jesus, I take authority over the money I need." (I called out the specific amount.) "I command you to come to me in Jesus' name."'[35] What a contrast with Jesus himself, who had 'nowhere to lay his head' (Matthew 8.20, Luke 9.58), but who promised a permanent dwelling *They have recast the promise of blessing back into the very form from which Jesus transformed it* 'in my Father's house' (John 14.2). This was typical of his teaching, in which success was defined not in terms of wealth in this life—indeed, the promised 'hundredfold return' comes just a few verses after his warning, 'How hard it is for the rich to enter the kingdom of God!' (Mark 10.23)—but in terms of treasure in heaven. In an ironic twist, prosperity teachers have thus recast the promise of blessing in the very form from which Jesus himself had transformed it. They have changed it from something to look forward to in the next life back into something to be 'named and claimed' here and now.

This is not a mistake we find in the rest of the New Testament. James, for instance, asks 'Has not God chosen those who are poor in the eyes of the world to be rich in faith and to inherit the kingdom?' (2.5), and warns against the corrosiveness of wealth (5.1–6) and the poison of covetousness (4.2). Paul similarly warns Timothy against the desire to get rich, telling him instead to 'Take hold of the eternal life to which you were called' (1 Timothy 6.6–12). Jesus' words to the church in Laodicea sum up the whole theme well: those who think they are rich and believe they need nothing, may in fact be 'wretched, pitiful, poor, blind and naked' in the eyes of God (Revelation 3.17). Success in the New Testament is thus measured by the acquisition not of worldly wealth but of a heavenly treasure, which may well be earned 'with persecutions.'

Greatness and Servanthood

A second strand in Jesus' teaching related to success is the theme of greatness. Jesus told his followers surprisingly often how to achieve greatness in the kingdom. The context reveals that this was partly because it was a question which preoccupied them. For example, in Matthew 18.1–4 they explicitly asked Jesus, 'Who is the greatest in the kingdom of heaven?' More often, however, the context was an argument among the twelve as to which of them was the greatest (Mark 9.34; Luke 9.46; 22.24). It is surely no coincidence that the first such dispute arose after the transfiguration, when Jesus chose just Peter, James and John to accompany him up the mountain, while the other nine found themselves unable to cure an epileptic boy. It is not hard to imagine how jealousy and rivalry might have strained relationships between the specially selected trio and the nine left-behind failures.[36]

James and John did not help matters when they later requested—either directly or through the agency of their mother—the privilege of sitting either side of Jesus in his kingdom (Matthew 20.20–4; Mark 10.35–41). The disciples were no different from anyone else; they wanted celebrity status. Garrison Keillor speaks for many church leaders when he expresses our deep-seated but rarely admitted hunger for approval:

> Under this thin veneer of modesty lies a monster of greed. I drive away faint praise, beating my little chest, waiting to be named Sun-God, King of America, Idol of Millions, Bringer of Fire, The Great Haji, Thun-Dar the Boy Giant. I do not want to say, 'Thanks, glad you liked it.' I want to say, 'Rise my people. Remove your faces from the carpet, stand, look me in the face.'[37]

But just as in the case of prosperity, Jesus turns the desire for greatness on its head. He tells the disciples that the way to greatness in the kingdom is by being the least: 'The greatest among you will be your servant. For whoever exalts himself will be humbled, and whoever humbles himself will be exalted' (Matthew 23.11–12; also Matthew 18.3–4; 20.25–8; Mark 10.42–5; Luke 9.48; 14.7–11; 18.9–14; 22.25–7). To exemplify greatness he stands a child in their midst, in the first century not so much a symbol of humility or innocence as of weakness and powerlessness.[38] In Robert Farrar Capon's memorable phrase, they were among 'the last, the least, the lost, the little and the dead,' life's losers who alone have the keys to the kingdom.[39] And to demonstrate in the most graphic form what he means, Jesus kneels before his followers and washes their feet (John 13.3–17). Yet even this is not the last or greatest act of servanthood that Jesus performs. As Paul puts it, 'He made himself nothing, taking the very nature of a servant, being made in human likeness. And being found in appearance as a man, he humbled himself and became obedient to death—even death on a cross' (Philippians 2.7–8). In the topsy-turvy world of the kingdom, greatness means humility.

In the topsy-turvy world of the kingdom greatness means humility

If one consequence of Jesus' redefinition of greatness is that it leaves no room for pride, another is that it also excludes competitiveness. That was the motive behind the disciples' arguments, and Jesus cut the ground from under their feet. We see it, too, in the complaint of John the Baptist's followers: 'Rabbi, that man who was with you on the other side of the Jordan—the one you testified about—well, he is baptizing, and everyone is going to him' (John 3.26). John's response is a model to us: 'He must become greater; I must become less' (3.30). This is true humility, which, as Jesus tells the crowd, is the path to true greatness: 'I tell you: among those born of women there is no-one greater than John' (Luke 7.28).[40] And yet competitiveness is a trap into which individual Christians, church leaders and indeed whole congregations continue to fall. Paul faced it in the church in Corinth, responding in terms which echo the words of Jesus in John 4: 'The man who plants and the man who waters have one purpose, and each will be rewarded according to his own labour' (3.8). The problem was a series of factions in the church, each championing their favourite teachers (1.12), but just a few years later the same problem manifested itself in a different way, this time in the form of various newly-arrived 'apostles' who compared Paul's ministry unfavourably with their own (2 Corinthians 10–13). On this occasion Paul took a different tack, refusing to be drawn into comparisons (2 Corinthians 10.12). They wanted to boast about their success and greatness; as we saw earlier, Paul's response was to boast of his weakness. This was fully in line with the teaching of Jesus: 'For it is not the one who commends himself who is approved, but the one whom the Lord commends' (2 Cor 10.18).

They wanted to boast about their success; Paul's response was to boast of his weakness

In the New Testament the whole concept of greatness is thus redefined, like that of wealth, from an eternal perspective. Greatness in the kingdom derives from humility and service, following the example of Jesus, not from status or superiority. And as with the promise of treasure in heaven, it will only be at the consummation of the kingdom that such true and lasting success will be revealed.

5 Jesus Redefines Success (2): Growth and Victory

A further form of success which Jesus refers to in his teaching can be summed up under the twin headings of fruitfulness and growth.

Although closely linked, there is a distinction between the two. Growth is the process of development and maturation, both in the individual and in the kingdom, while fruitfulness is reproduction and multiplication. An example of the former is the parable of the mustard seed, which starts small, but grows and grows (Matthew 13.31–2; Mark 4.30–2; Luke 13.18–19). An illustration of the latter is the parable of the sower, in which the initial frustrations of fruitlessness lead in the end to incredible yields—thirty, sixty, even a hundred fold (Matthew 13.3–9; Mark 4.3–9; Luke 8.5–8). Obviously there can be an overlap between the two, since growth should lead to fruitfulness, and fruitfulness makes the kingdom grow. The image of the vine incorporates both images; the implicit message is one of growth, the explicit expectation 'that you bear much fruit' (John 15.1–8). At the same time there is a warning, which is also echoed in the parable of the fig tree (Luke 13.6–9) and the cursing of the same (Matthew 21.19; Mark 11.13–14, 20–1), that fruitlessness is not acceptable to God. We are called to be fruitful and expected to succeed. Having said that, the way to fruitfulness is to 'remain in the vine'—it is God who gives the growth, not our effort. This is brought out even more clearly in the parable of the growing seed (Mark 4.26–9).

Fruitlessness is not acceptable to God; we are called to be fruitful

The growth which Jesus describes is not only the extension of the kingdom, as in the parable of the mustard seed, but also the maturation of the individual, the spiritual growth of the disciple. Jesus expected his followers to grow in holiness: 'Be perfect, therefore, as your heavenly Father is perfect' (Matthew 5.48). This is meant to encourage rather than discourage us, even if it sometimes has the opposite effect! It will show itself in our seeking to live out the Sermon on the Mount, by being poor in spirit, meek, merciful, pure in heart, and so forth (5.1–9), by 'letting [our] light shine before others' (5.16) and by having a 'righteousness [which] surpasses that of the Pharisees and the teachers of the law' (5.20). This is a fruitfulness which cannot be measured in numerical terms, but which produces the kind of fruit of which Paul speaks in Galatians 5.22–3, the fruit of the Spirit. Unlike the previous two forms of kingdom 'success' we have considered, this one is apparent in this life as well as in the age to come, albeit not always to the individual who is growing.

Another kind of fruitfulness can be seen in a well-known incident at the start of Jesus' ministry. The disciples went fishing, and after a fruitless night, Jesus told them where to cast their nets, as a result of which they met with tremendous success. But this is no endorsement of the prosperity gospel, 'follow Jesus and get rich quick.' No, as soon as they came ashore Jesus said to Simon, 'From now on you will bring in people instead of fish,' and they pulled their boats up on shore, left everything and followed him (Luke 5.1–12, CEV). This fruitfulness—God-given success—thus led to a call to work with God for greater fruitfulness in his harvest field.

Harvesting the Crop

This theme of a crop to be harvested is itself found at various points in Jesus' teaching. 'I tell you, open your eyes and look at the fields! They are ripe for harvest. Even now the reaper draws his wages, even now he harvests the crop for eternal life, so that the sower and the reaper may be glad together. Thus the saying "One sows and another reaps" is true. I sent you to reap what you have not worked for. Others have done the hard work, and you have reaped the benefits of their labour' (John 4.35–8; also Matthew 9.37–8; Luke 10.2). I have quoted these verses in full because they echo the point made earlier that success in the kingdom is collaborative rather than competitive. On this occasion, at Sychar, Jesus sowed the seed and the disciples reaped the fruit. The success which they enjoyed was the result of his work, and consequently no cause for pride on their part.

Success in the kingdom is collaborative not competitive

The twin themes of fruitfulness and growth are particularly prevalent in Acts, where Luke reports with obvious delight the conversion of about 3000 people on the day of Pentecost, growth to 5000 men a little later, and the continuing growth and spread of the church thereafter (2.41; 4.4; 12.24; 14.21; 19.20). Luke was evidently not afraid to 'play the numbers game' because he saw the growth of the church as the success of the gospel. At the same time, however, the glory went not to himself nor indeed to any of the apostles, but solely to God. Paul's letters similarly reflect his heart's desire to see the 'gospel...bearing fruit and growing,' and Christians 'bearing fruit in every good work, growing in the knowledge of God' (Colossians 1.6, 10). Yet Paul also made plain that such success could be costly, in that it often involved suffering, for 'suffering produces perseverance; perseverance, character; and character, hope' (Romans 5.3–4). This was not only Paul's own experience, but also that of the early church in general. James and Peter thus likewise testified that personal growth often comes through trials (James 1.2–4; 1 Peter 1.6–9), while Luke noted that the growth of the church came through persecution, as the scattered believers took the gospel to more and more places (Acts 8.1–4).

Victory

The fourth strand of success in Jesus' teaching is that of victory in the spiritual realm, which takes two quite distinct forms.

On the one hand there is Jesus' teaching about his future vindication, the victory of the cross, which we considered above. Tom Wright's words offer a concise summary: '[Jesus] had come to see the cross in deeply symbolic terms: symbolic of…the way of defeat which he had announced as the way of victory…It was to become the symbol, because it was the means, of the victory of God.'[41] As we said earlier, the cross once again redefines success, as victory comes through apparent defeat, and vindication through death. This repeats the final point of the previous section, that suffering can be God's chosen path to glory.

The second aspect of Jesus' teaching about victory can be found in various references to spiritual conflict. For example, he said that in his ministry he was 'binding the strong man and robbing his house' (Matthew 12.29; Mark 3.27; Luke 11.21–2). Similarly, when his disciples returned from a mission he exclaimed: 'I saw Satan fall like lightning from heaven' (Luke 10.18). But what lay behind these images of triumph? In the former case, the context was a discussion about Jesus' exorcisms; in the latter, the seventy-two had been sent out with the instructions, 'Heal the sick who are there and tell them, "The kingdom of God is near you,"' and they had returned saying, 'Lord, even the demons submit to us in your name' (Luke 10.1–17). In other words, their victory consisted of preaching the gospel, healing the sick and casting out demons (Matthew 10; Mark 3.14–15; [16.17–18]; Luke 9.1–6).

Their victory consisted of preaching the gospel, healing the sick and casting out demons

This ties in with the 'manifesto' with which Jesus launched his ministry, according to Luke (4.18–19), and the 'great commission' with which he ended it, according to Matthew (28.19–20). Given that the followers of Jesus are still called to live out that manifesto and that commission, we, too, are evidently fighting a spiritual battle. Not that this will always lead to easy victories.

Jesus warned his disciples that there would also be times of rejection, when they had to wipe the dust of a town off their feet (Matthew 10.14; Luke 9.5; 10.10). But that rejection should not be taken personally, since whoever rejects Jesus' disciple rejects him (Luke 10.16). If success offers no grounds for boasting, failure gives no cause for despair.

If success offers no grounds for boasting, failure gives no cause for despair

When we turn to the rest of the New Testament, the theme of victory in the spiritual realm is a little more prominent than in the teaching of Jesus. Revelation in particular describes at length the church's spiritual battle and the ultimate victory of God. It also contains references to individual victories to be won; each of the letters to the seven churches includes a promise to 'the one who overcomes' (or 'conquers': 2.7, 11, 17, 26; 3.5, 12, 21; see also 21.7). Yet a closer look reveals that the victories in Revelation are of both types which Jesus describes. While Christ is portrayed as 'a conqueror bent on conquest' (5.2), for his followers victory may come through the apparent 'defeat' of the martyr's death (12.11; 15.2). As Ladd comments, 'This victory is not a physical or worldly one; it is a victory analogous to the victory won by Christ himself, even though it involved his death on the cross.'[42]

This is what it means to be 'more than conquerors' even in the midst of 'trouble, hardship, persecution, famine, nakedness, danger and the sword' (Romans 8.36–8). As we saw with poverty and prosperity and with servanthood and status, what appears to be failure or weakness in the eyes of the world may be success in God's sight. At the same time, there are victories to be won in the daily spiritual conflict. For, as John says, 'The one who is in you is greater than the one who is in the world' (1 John 4.4). In its context, this refers primarily to the victory of the truth of the gospel over false teaching; elsewhere John mentions victory over temptation (1 John 5.4).[43] This in turn is all thanks to the topsy-turvy victory of the cross, which has, as Paul says, given us victory over the power of sin and death (1 Corinthians 15.57).

6

So What?

While it is good, indeed important, to look at what the Bible has to say about success, it is equally important to ask the question: so what?

As one curate's wife used to say after her husband had faithfully expounded Scripture but rather skimped on the application: 'What use is that to me on Monday morning?' Or as a colleague helpfully put it during the writing of this booklet: 'So we have got the map which shows us where to go, but now how do we get there?'

First of all, we have seen that in a society which worships material prosperity, Jesus commands us to worship God and to invest in heaven's treasures. This means having a mindset at odds with the materialistic consumerism of our age. It means believing that 'a person's life does not consist in the abundance of their possessions' (Luke 12.16), in defiance of the claims of the advertising agencies. In a society where 6-year-olds are teased for not wearing the right brand of trainers, this is profoundly counter-cultural and will not be easy.

In a society where 6-year-olds are teased for not wearing the right brand of trainers, this is profoundly counter-cultural

Furthermore, given the context of much of Jesus' teaching on the subject, it also means giving generously to God's work and to the poor, rediscovering the freedom that being a 'cheerful giver' brings. Perhaps surprisingly, this does not necessarily exclude worldly 'success.' Such household names as the construction giant Sir John Laing, J L Kraft of the Kraft Cheese Corporation and William Colgate the toothpaste manufacturer all reached the top of their professions, but all gave away huge sums, far more than a tenth of what they earned. Indeed, when Sir John Laing died, his estate amounted to just £371. These men understood that in Jesus' redefined terms success is measured not by our bank balance or our lifestyle, but by what we do with what we have got.

Similarly, we have been reminded that in a society which idolizes status, Jesus tells us to be the servant of all. This again impacts first and foremost on our mindset, warning us to beware the subtle yet powerful ambition which wants to be looked up to, to be seen to be successful. Richard Exley is typical of many church leaders when he confesses,

> My predominant concern was "How can I build a bigger church?" rather than "How can I be a more faithful minister of Jesus Christ?" The determining factor in my decision-making was not, "Is this God's will?" but "How will this look on my résumé?"[44]

For many lay people the struggle is the same, even if its outward form may be different.

The first step towards conquering this pride (for that is essentially what it is) is the recognition of our mixed motives. We then need to learn to measure our success not by our achievements or our reputation, but by the growth of our relationship with God. Richard Exley continues, 'I learned to base my success on my relationship with Jesus. With God's help I set new goals—character and spiritual goals.' There are practical strategies we can adopt to help us in this. John Ortberg helpfully lists three—the disciplines of solitude, accountability and secrecy.[45] Solitude helps us to see ourselves, our successes and our failures, in an eternal perspective. Being accountable to another, whether a spiritual director or a trusted friend, helps us to be honest with ourselves and with God. And the discipline of secrecy (being 'careful not to do your acts of righteousness before others, to be seen by them'—Matthew 6.1) helps us to do right for God's sake, not to look good.

Success is measured by what we do with what we have got

Called not Driven

If we can manage to wean ourselves off the approval of others and conquer our addiction to status, it can have some very beneficial side-effects. For a start, it means that we will begin to live as those who are called rather than driven. In his book *Ordering Your Private World* Gordon MacDonald lists the characteristics of a driven person, and it is not a pretty sight: constant busyness, volcanic anger, broken relationships, ethical shortcuts,[46] and, we might add, ulcers, heart problems, nervous breakdown and an early grave.

We will begin to live as those who are called rather than driven

A driven person is never satisfied, never fulfilled, never at peace. We surely want to know God's calling and pursue that, rather than to be driven by the desperate need for approval and success.

Furthermore, this can and should do wonders for our self-esteem. So many people in our society, including many Christians, base their level of self-worth on other people's opinions and expectations. As Arabella Weir's novel anxiously asks: 'Does my bum look big in this?' Yet if we gauge success not by our appearance, our job, our bank balance or, indeed, by how big our church is, but by God's approval then we can be free indeed. Richard Exley concludes:

> 'For the first time in my life, I felt liberated. The work of the ministry still needed to be done, but now it was the by-product of my relationship with the Lord, an expression of who I was in him, rather than an attempt to prove my worth. I felt content, rather than competitive, and for the first time rejoiced genuinely in the achievements of my peers.'[47]

The Cancer of Competition

This brings out a third benefit that we touched on earlier: it cuts out the cancer of competitiveness. We begin to recognize that everyone is called to different tasks: one to sow, another to reap; one to plant, another to water. One is called to preach to great crowds and to see the most amazing results as they turn to God in repentance (Jonah 3). Another is called to preach his heart out and to see the people walk away, grumbling, 'This is a hard teaching. Who can accept it?' (John 6.60–6). One apparent 'success,' one apparent 'failure,' but both fulfilling the will of God, and so both enjoying God's approval (even if, ironically, the 'successful' one still was not happy!) As Richard Exley says, if we can recognize our different callings, it can liberate us to affirm others in their successes. Instead of comparing ourselves with them and feeling that we have to minimize their accomplishments and maximize our own, we can recognize that we are called to one task and they to another. As someone once said to the Scripture Union schools' worker who brought me to Christ: 'If God has called you to be a children's worker, don't stoop to becoming Archbishop of Canterbury!'

If God has called you to be a children's worker, don't stoop to becoming Archbishop of Canterbury!

This naturally relates to the question of growth and fruitfulness. If we stop measuring ourselves against the achievements of others, and instead focus on nurturing our own relationship with God and prayerfully seeking to follow his calling for our lives, our own successes and failures will be put in a different perspective. For example, at Meribah Moses seemed to score a resounding success, bringing water gushing from the rock, yet in God's eyes it was Moses' disobedience which was ultimately of greater significance (Numbers 20.1–13). Kent and Barbara Hughes comment, 'This tremendous lesson from the life of Moses teaches us that one can be regarded as hugely success-ful in the ministry and yet be a failure.'[48] On the other hand, real or apparent failures can be growth points in our relationship with God and in our fruit-fulness for him. Take Peter, for instance. His experience of denial, broken-ness and failure made him not weaker but stronger as a leader. Or to take a different example, on the surface it would appear that missionaries like Henry Martyn or Jim Elliott were failures, yet the fruitfulness of their lives and deaths for Christ has been incalculable.

Judging by Kingdom Criteria

This acceptance of the place of failure in our lives does not mean lapsing into a typically British 'Dunkirk mentality,' which makes heroes out of dis-astrous ski jumpers or hopeless swimmers. Rather, it means judging by king-dom criteria. As we saw earlier, John the Baptist had to watch as the crowds deserted him and flocked to Jesus. Yet he could see that this was God's plan, and that ultimately greater fruitfulness would ensue. And so, however diffi-cult it must have been, he embraced his calling, saying, 'A man can receive only what is given him from heaven' (John 3.27).

Part of the key here is to see things, as John did, from a long-term perspec-tive, in a world which thinks overwhelmingly in the short term. To use one of the New Testament images mentioned earlier, we are running a mara-thon, not a sprint. Don Carson tells the story of his father's ministry as a church-planter in Quebec. It was a long hard slog with very little fruit, and during the years Mr Carson senior was there, numerous other evangelists came and went. But God had given him a vision of fruitfulness, and by God's grace he lived long enough to see a wonderful harvest.[49] Jesus' para-bles of growth remind us that growth takes time. If we need further convincing, think of Jesus' own life; how 'successful' was his ministry in all those years as a car-

How 'successful' was Jesus' ministry in all those years as a carpenter?

penter? We can only presume that Jesus knew God's timing, and that those 'missing' years were preparation for the ministry to which he was called. We need to learn patience, a key aspect of spiritual fruitfulness (Galatians 5.22). Ironically, this can be especially hard for those who want to do great things for God. Richard Exley hits the nail on the head when he says, citing David's ambition to build the temple, 'We are not tempted to do bad things as much as we are tempted to try things God has not called us to.'[50]

The Pitfalls of Success

Having said this, we must not forget that success, too, has its own pitfalls. For it brings with it temptations to pride, sloth and ingratitude, to name but three.[51] Success can distort our perspective, and like power, tend to corrupt. Richard Higginson cites the example of Solomon, whose wisdom and wealth were legendary, but whose many foreign wives led to the neglect of his relationship with God, which in turn led to the division of the kingdom.[52] So when the seventy-two came back flushed with victory, Jesus warned them: 'Do not rejoice that the spirits submit to you, but rejoice that your names are written in heaven' (Luke 10.20). In other words, do

A good sports player thinks about the game, not about how well he or she is playing

not get so carried away with your spiritual success that you forget the most important thing, your relationship with the Father.

Knute Larson offers some helpful tips on how to avoid the seduction of success, particularly spiritual success. Keep working hard, making sure we do not neglect the mundane and routine. Be generous with praise, giving thanks not only to God but also to others. Be patient, not allowing ourselves to be driven by a compulsion for greater success. Do not focus on the success. A good sports player thinks about the game, not about how well he or she is playing. Stay humble, remembering where we came from, and who it is who has given us the success we enjoy. Last but most definitely not least, keep praying, to maintain our daily closeness to God. He closes with a very apt quotation from Corrie ten Boom. When asked how she handled people's acclamation, she said, 'Well, I take the flowers, and I thank the people, and I enjoy the flowers a little bit. Then each evening, I put them in a bunch and give them back to the Lord where they belong.'[53]

Giving it all back to the Lord is the only way to cope with failure and to handle success

Giving it all back to the Lord, where it belongs is, it seems to me, the only way to get the right perspective on success, to cope with failure and to handle success. As we keep our eyes on him we learn to store up treasure in heaven rather than focus on material prosperity, to be servants rather than worry about status. As we keep our eyes on him we want to grow and be fruitful, and to see the kingdom grow and bear fruit. As we live out our calling, using the gifts we have been given, we look forward in hope to that day when we, too, hear those wonderful words, 'Well done, good and faithful servant.'

Notes

1   Dietrich Bonhoeffer, *Ethics* (SCM, 1955) p 15.
2   See for example Kent and Barbara Hughes' excellent book, *Liberating Ministry from the Success Syndrome* (Tyndale House, 1987) p 35.
3   Tom Wright, *Bringing the Church to the World* (Bethany House, 1992) p 185 (published in the UK as *New Tasks for a Renewed Church*).
4   Richard Higginson, *Transforming Leadership* (SPCK, 1996) p 112.
5   Roland Howard, *Charismania* (Mowbray, 1997) p 126. Although Howard does not single out Alpha for criticism, he is negative towards Holy Trinity Brompton, and extremely critical of March for Jesus.
6   Kenneth Hagin, *New Thresholds of Faith* (Faith Library, 1980) pp 54–5, quoted in Dan McConnell, *The Promise of Health and Wealth* (Hodder and Stoughton, 1990) p 175.
7   Maria Boulding, *Gateway to Hope: an Exploration of Failure* (Fount, 1985) pp 37–57, at p 37. See also Russ Parker, *Free to Fail* (Triangle, 1992) pp 57–8.
8   Norman C Habel, *The Book of Job* (OTL, SCM, 1985) p 585; see also J Gerald Janzen, *Job* (Interpretation, John Knox Press, 1985) p 267 and D Atkinson, *The Message of Job* (BST, IVP, 1991) pp 159–61.
9   McConnell, *Promise of Health and Wealth*, p 162.
10 *ibid*, p 163.
11 Robert Davidson, *Ecclesiastes and Song of Solomon* (DSB, St Andrew Press, 1986) p 15.
12 John R O'Neil, *The Paradox of Success: When Winning at Work becomes Losing at Life* (McGraw-Hill, 1995).
13 P W L Walker puts it succinctly: 'Within Christian theology it is…illegitimate to approach the Old Testament text as though the New Testament had not been written': *Jesus and the Holy City* (Eerdmans, 1996) p 313.
14 Jacques Ellul, *Money and Power* (Marshall Pickering, 1986) pp 71–2.
15 Boulding, *Gateway to Hope*, p 71.
16 Paul Tournier, *The Person Reborn* (SCM, 1977) p 33, quoted in Parker, *Free to Fail*, p 73.
17 See for example N T Wright, *The New Testament and the People of God* (Fortress, 1992) pp 388–9 and *Jesus and the Victory of God* (Fortress, 1996), pp 167–8.
18 Boulding, *Gateway to Hope*, pp 25, 30–32.
19 *Ibid*, p 72.
20 The words are those of Markus Bockmuehl in a chapter entitled 'Did Jesus Fail?' in *This Jesus: Martyr, Lord, Messiah* (IVP, 1996) p 77.
21 Walter Moberly, 'Proclaiming Christ crucified: some reflections on the use and abuse of the Gospels,' *Anvil* 5.1 (1988) pp 31–52, here at p 39.
22 Even so, in my experience Good Friday services almost invariably adopt the Markan or Matthean tone of dereliction and despair rather than the more positive perspective of Luke or John.
23 See for example Morna D Hooker, *The Message of Mark* (Epworth, 1983) chap 1.
24 Bockmuehl's very different approach to the question, 'Did Jesus fail?,' looking in terms of Jesus' own frame of reference, similarly concludes, 'His death did not mean he failed': *This Jesus*, p 97.
25 Robert Schuller, *Living Positively One Day at a Time* (Fleming H Revell, 1981) p 201, quoted in Parker, *Free to Fail*, p 20.

26 McConnell, *Promise of Health and Wealth*, p 178; David Prior, *Jesus and Power* (IVP, 1987) p 48.

27 Boulding, *Gateway to Hope*, p 90; see also Parker, *Free to Fail*, p 59.

28 Bauer, Arndt and Gingrich's *Lexicon* offers both as translations of the Greek term Paul uses, *kateirgasato*.

29 Fred Smith, 'Granting permission to succeed,' in Marshall Shelley (ed), *Empowering Your Church Through Creativity and Change* (Moorings, 1995) p 213.

30 See the helpful discussion in Gordon Fee, *The First Epistle to the Corinthians* (NICNT, Eerdmans, 1987) pp 136–45, esp p 143.

31 Which, as Wenham says, 'should be regarded as pictorial rather than as anything like a literal description of heaven and hell. The parable was not intended as a map of the after-life, though it has often been used or misused in that way': David Wenham, *The Parables of Jesus* (Hodder and Stoughton, 1989) pp 144–5.

32 Although this concept was present in other Jewish literature of the time, that does not enlighten us as to what the disciples understood by it: see for example Donald A Carson, 'Matthew' in *Expositors' Bible Commentary 8* (Zondervan, 1984) p 177, with references.

33 John R W Stott, *Christian Counter-culture: The Message of the Sermon on the Mount* (BST, IVP, 1978) p 156.

34 Gloria Copeland, *God's Will is Prosperity* (Harrison House, 1978), p 54, quoted in McConnell, *Promise of Health and Wealth*, p 172.

35 Copeland, *God's Will is Prosperity*, pp 48–9, quoted in Dave Hunt and T A McMahon, *The Seduction of Christianity* (Harvest House, 1985) p 101.

36 I owe this insight to Prior, *Jesus and Power*, pp 81–2.

37 Garrison Keillor, *Lake Wobegon Days* (Faber and Faber, 1989) p 263.

38 'A child was a person of no importance in Jewish society, subject to the authority of his elders, not taken seriously except as a responsibility, one to be looked after, not looked up to': R T France, *Matthew* (TNTC, IVP, 1985) p 270.

39 Robert Farrar Capon, *The Parables of Grace* (Eerdmans, 1988) pp 17, 32–4.

40 Although Jesus continued, 'yet the one who is least in the kingdom of God is greater than he,' I take this not as diminishing the greatness of John, the last and greatest of the prophets, but rather as highlighting the even greater glory of the kingdom which was being inaugurated: see for example Robert H Stein, *Luke* (NAC, Broadman, 1992) p 230, or Joel B Green, *The Gospel of Luke* (NICNT, Eerdmans, 1997) p 299.

41 Wright, *Jesus and the Victory of God*, p 610.

42 George Eldon Ladd, *A Commentary on the Revelation of John* (Eerdmans, 1972) pp 40–1.

43 That the 'world' here represents the temptations of the world can be inferred from 2.15–16: see I Howard Marshall, *The Epistles of John* (NICNT, Eerdmans, 1978) pp 228–9.

44 Richard Exley, 'Taming Ambition' in Richard Exley, Mark Galli and John Ortberg, *Dangers, Toils and Snares* (Multnomah, 1994) p 48.

45 John Ortberg, 'Breaking the approval addiction,' in *Dangers, Toils and Snares*, pp 31–40.

46 Gordon MacDonald, *Ordering Your Private World* (second UK edition, Highland, 1987) pp 32–8.

47 Exley, 'Taming Ambition,' pp 49–50.

48 Hughes and Hughes, *Liberating Ministry from the Success Syndrome*, p 36.

49 D A Carson, *A Call to Spiritual Reformation* (Baker and IVP, 1992) pp 154–5.

50 Exley, 'Taming Ambition,' p 43.

51 See Daniel Jenkins, *Christian Maturity and the Theology of Success* (SCM, 1976) p 3.

52 Higginson, *Transforming Leadership*, p 113.

53 Knute Larson, 'When things are going well,' in Stuart Briscoe, Knute Larson and Larry Osborne, *Measuring Up: The Need to Succeed and the Fear of Failure* (Multnomah, 1993) pp 134–7.